**Coal**

# The Coal Anthology

Edited by Ann Sansom, Peter Sansom
and Sarah Wimbush

smith|doorstop

# the poetry business

Published 2024
by The Poetry Business
Campo House,
54 Campo Lane,
Sheffield S1 2EG
www.poetrybusiness.co.uk

Copyright © The Contributors 2024
The moral rights of the author have been asserted.
ISBN 978-1-914914-89-4

All rights reserved.
Without limiting the rights under copyright reserved above, no part of this publication may be reproduced, storied in or introduced into a retrieval system, or transmitted, in any form or by any means (electronic, mechanical, photocopying, recording or otherwise), without the prior written permission of both the copyright owner and the above publisher of this book.

With many thanks to the National Coal Mining Museum, ncm.org.uk

Designed & typeset by Utter
Cover design by Pete Hebden
Printed by Imprint Digital

British Library Cataloguing-in-Publication Data.
A catalogue record for this book is available from the British Library.

Smith|Doorstop is a member of Inpress
www.inpressbooks.co.uk.

Distributed by BookSource, 50 Cambuslang Road,
Cambuslang Investment Park, Glasgow G32 8NB.

The Poetry Business gratefully acknowledges the support
of Arts Council England.

# Contents

| | | |
|---|---|---|
| 10 | **Barnsley Miner** | Sue Riley |
| 11 | **Black Country** | Liz Berry |
| 12 | **Bolero** | M W Bewick |
| 13 | **Box of White** | Stuart Pickford |
| 14 | **Brass Rubbing on a School Trip** | Laura Strickland |
| 14 | **Brassed Off** | Zoë Walkington |
| 16 | **Breezeblock** | Jonathan Edwards |
| 18 | **Buried truth** | Lesley Curwen |
| 20 | **Buying a Bike** | Lesley Ingram |
| 21 | **Clover** | Jeanette Burton |
| 23 | **Coal** | Brian McCabe |
| 24 | **Coal** | Julie Sheridan |
| 25 | **The Coal Faces** | Gordon Dargie |
| 26 | **Coal Picking, Broomhill** | Ian McMillan |
| 27 | **Credo** | Rachel Burns |
| 28 | **Dad, 83** | Alison Tanik |
| 30 | **The Daughter of a Scab** | Rachel Moore |
| 30 | **Deputy Stick** | Tracy Dawson |
| 32 | **Digging With My Grandfather: John Richard Evans (19 July 1880 – 9 September 1957)** | Elaine Oswald |
| 35 | **Down Pit** | Jane Burn |
| 36 | **Every Man was Singing** | David Amos |
| 38 | **Ferrybridge Blues** | Liz McPherson |
| 39 | **First-Aider, Oakdale Colliery** | David Thomas |
| 42 | **The Flower Arranger** | Alan Payne |
| 43 | **Frost-Gods** | Harold Massingham |
| 46 | **I Have Loved Coal** | Emily Cotterill |
| 48 | **'I thought I might tell you my story'** | Adrian Buttree |
| 52 | **In the Boat House** | John Whitehouse |

| | |
|---|---|
| 53 | **Jam Butty** John Chambers |
| 54 | **Left Behind** Katharine Goda |
| 58 | **Lisa's Homework** Joe Williams |
| 59 | **Memorial** David Harmer |
| 61 | **Mining** Harriet Torr |
| 63 | **Most likely a Part of Astley Deep** Steven Taylor |
| 64 | *from* **All Hell Broke Loose – the Miners' Strike, the Battle of Orgreave and the Consequences** John Harris |
| 69 | **Pit Closure as a Tarantino Short** Helen Mort |
| 70 | **Pneumoconiosis** Duncan Bush |
| 71 | **The Queue** Robbie Burton |
| 72 | **Scargill** Sarah Wimbush |
| 73 | **Thatcher** Ian Parks |
| 74 | **Scuttle** Simon Armitage |
| 76 | **Six Bells** Gillian Clarke |
| 77 | **Shopping List** Safa Maryam |
| 78 | **1984** Pam Thompson |
| 80 | **Stone** Audrey Henderson |
| 81 | **Survey** Oliver Comins |
| 82 | **The Thread** Wayne Price |
| 83 | *from* **The Two Magicians** Paul Bentley |
| 85 | **Valley Funeral** Hilary Taylor |
| 86 | **Vigil** Judith Wozniak |
| 87 | **Wayside** Rosie Jackson |
| 90 | **You Have Got to Stand Somewhere** Keith Pattison |
| 92 | **Wound Up** John Foggin |
| | |
| 96 | **About the Contributors** |

With photographs by David Amos, John Harris, Keith Pattison, Brenda Price, John Robinson, Russell Smith, Harold White, Ken Wilkinson and Sarah Wimbush.

Photograph courtesy © Keith Pattison

# Barnsley Miner

His face familiar as the Town Hall clock,
his forehead the grit of Wharncliffe Crags.
His eyes black diamonds, hard and bright,
the changing lights of Stairfoot roundabout.

His gut is a corfe of nuggets, his tendons
are seams of untapped Kents Thin.
His hewer's hands are Albert Hirst black puddings,
his battered cod feet wrapped in yesterday's Sun.

He worships each Sunday at the Alhambra Centre,
retreats thereafter to the allotment loft;
his prayers are on wings; he releases the flock
to circle and home in at his call.

His blood is the dark Barnsley Bitter,
his spinal fluid's the Don & Dearne.
His brain's the Welfare, the Grimethorpe
Band his sounding brass tradition.

His head the height of Locke Park Tower
his back turned for ever on Arthur's Castle,
his heartbeat's The Reds, and his mantra the chants
in the Spion Kop end at Oakwell.

   Sue Riley

# Black Country

Commuters saw it first, vast
on the hillside by the A41,
a wingless Pegasus, hooves
kicking road into the distance.

It had appeared overnight.
A black shadow on the scrub,
galloping over the gates
of the derelict factories,

facing East, towards the pits,
mouth parted as if it would
swallow the sun that rose
from behind the winding gear.

Word spread. Crowds gathered.
Kids, someone said,
but when they examined the flanks
they found pure coal,

coal where none had been mined
in years, where houses
still collapsed into empty shafts
and hills bore scars.

A gift from the underworld,
hauling the past
from the dead earth. Old men
knelt to breathe the smoke

of its mane, whisper
in its ear, walked away
in silence, fists clenched,
faces streaked with tears.

   Liz Berry

# Bolero

With Tommy Cooper's curtain call
the start of Greenham common evictions
come with colliery men watching their
unravelling to the sound of Ravel.

I pick a sack of heavy news
from the village Postie's grubby floor
and head out to the rain of my daily round
and the stain of print on me la'al fingers.

A box of Frosties, a formica table,
a pencil case and a Rexel folder
in a Smiths carrier, the older lads
with their Regals at the back of the bus.

The marras of Whitehaven already done for,
pits inked for closure before the headlines,
before Virgin Atlantic, Thames Barrier,
the glossy Orwell pop of our own 84.

And the top-deck rocks as we pass the cemetery,
the iron bridge of the disused railway,
waiting for kids to get on board for schooling,
looking down to the top of the flaking shelter
there's a spray-paint word we'll allus remember

And the word we remember is SCAB.

   MW Bewick

# Box of White

Grandad Jack hangs his bait from a beam
to stop it twitching with mice.
In his tin that snaps shut, he has an onion
and lumps of bread. As the men make off
to find a spot to squat in the dark,
he scoops in concrete powder, sneaks out
that box of white past the deputy.

Lamps give patterns to the fossils.
Every Sunday, he tips it all out,
pulls away the centre with a shovel
and feeds the thirsty circle sips of water,
folding in the outer rim to thicken,
take up the weight and gloss. Each batch,
*he tamps out the fat*; another page,
another smooth step to the greenhouse
he'd built from old timbers and glass,
strong enough to mimic all weathers.

Inside, he conjures up chrysanths,
tells Mum they're suns of November,
pompons that came from China long ago.
With nimble fingers, she picks out
any green or torn petals so they'll be
perfect for him at the Hersden Show.

Stuart Pickford

# Brass Rubbing on a School Trip

Michael Dunn knocks my hand and the crayon sends a red streak across the paper. Instead of starting again I keep going, I like the imperfection, the shock of colour across the words like they're burning. *Blaster,* the ex-miner, sticks our rubbings on a wall and as we huddle for our photo, shouts *say coal!* Later when I run towards the rec to play out, I use a stick to rattle the fence, sing *Coal Not Dole, Coal Not Dole, Coal Not Dole.*

Laura Strickland

# Brassed Off

It's about trumpets and cornets, but it isn't really, it's about coal. When he says *it's music that matters,* the old man that dies, the Pete Postlethwaite one, we're meant to think that the music is more important than the coal. At GCSE they might set you a question *Music is more important than coal. Discuss. Show your working.*

One of the actors, Stephen Tompkinson, plays a character that dresses as a children's entertainer called Mr. Chuckles. His huge overly long floppy shoes are huge shoes of despair. His wife thinks he's useless. That is because he is. His children have snotty noses, like everyone did in the '80s. Bailiffs come. A lot of snooker is played. To make us keep watching, Ewan McGregor falls in love with a girl who plays the flugelhorn. If it wasn't for that we'd have turned it off.

Zoë Walkington

Photograph courtesy © Russell Smith from The Last Man Standing project.

# Breezeblock

*'Two boys, Hancock and Shankland, had picked up a concrete post ... they flung it over the top and onto the dual carriageway and it killed the taxi driver who was taking the scabs into work in Merthyr Vale.'*
*– Phil Cullen, Brittle with Relics*

Let's make it happen
backwards, lift the breezeblock
from this smashed windscreen, raise it up
through air – nothing can do this
but time – the glass
reforming itself beneath it
until it's solid, smooth, the driver
whistling, as the car reverses
through the early traffic. Up
towards the flyover, where two men
stand, leaning
over the edge, watching the breezeblock
rush towards them, their arms out
to catch it. Let's have them
put the breezeblock safely down, relieved
to be rid of their burden, right here
on the bridge, share
a joke with each other, shake
hands, then head
backwards through the town, as the early
morning sky fills with stars. Outside
their doors, let them return
unlit cigarettes to jacket pockets
and step
into their houses, up the stairs, past
rooms where their children are sleeping,
into their own bedrooms, where they slip
under duvets. Later, they can come down –
nothing can do this
but words – to eggs, nothing special
on the radio news, a world going

the right way, a view of the morning
through innocent eyes. But now let's leave them
where they are for one more hour, snoring
straight through the alarm, arms
round their warm wives, under mortgaged roofs,
dreaming of a world
in which there is no strike.

  Jonathan Edwards

# Buried truth

Fast-food joints, supermarkets and shopping malls. That's all you can see now, a concrete wilderness, built on the bones of a once-thriving Manchester coalfield. It was an industry that had supported thousands of jobs and families but in a short few years it crumbled, and colliery sites were sold off for development.

I watched the rot setting in, from the sidelines, as a young reporter.

'Get over to Salford, and put your foot down!' was an order I'd heard before. Everyone in the Piccadilly Radio newsroom had. I dreaded it, because it meant taking the radio car, alone. I remember grabbing the keys and running upstairs to the roof car park.

It was 1984 and although Arthur Scargill had called a strike over pit closures, there had been no national ballot. This caused a bitter quarrel between different coalfields, collieries and even colleagues. In some of these pockets of resistance, men stubbornly continued working. Sometimes people changed sides.

In Manchester, I remember there was one local leader who defied the Scargill line. He became known in mining circles as 'Piccadilly Jim' because he gave us frequent interviews about the right of his men to do their shifts as normal. I can't recall his surname, but he was a large, forthright bloke who was convinced of his case. I must admit, he did enjoy the limelight.

Every time I drove to a working pit, my mind would be churning layers of expectation. I was a young and inexperienced journalist, and my particular horror was the operation to raise a massive aerial on the radio car, without hitting a bird or a power line. Dealing with a possibly violent crowd was low down the list of worries.

A useful landmark on approach were four massive brick chimneys which marked the pit site, and it was usual to see a scatter of men walking around, in grimy white helmets and orange overalls marked with coaldust.

At the pit gates, it was usually quiet, until the next shift of men arrived for work.

After forty years, my memories are not crystal clear. They're a series of impressions, of noise, of an electric charge in the air, a distillation of hatred, anger and despair.

On one occasion, flying pickets of striking Yorkshire miners arrived in scruffy coaches. Lines of burly men got out, and a cache of placards was unloaded. There was a dim skirl of sirens in the distance and police vans raced up, their blue lights whirling.

I remember carrying my UHER reel-to-reel tape recorder to the gates, where pickets were stationed. I pressed play and record and held out the large microphone. Men distributed placards and called friendly obscenities to do with the size of the mike, and the fact that my car was decorated with the station catchphrase 'Nobody Does It Better'. There was a rumble of heavy wheels and a bus hove into view, ferrying in working miners. An ear-splitting chorus broke out of 'scab, scab, scab!'.

The sound I gathered on shiny brown tape (swiftly edited with a razor) could never convey the emotions on that picket line. And the factual report I scribbled for the late bulletins, in a lined notebook, could not describe the complexity of what was happening.

I pressed the buttons to raise the aerial, and prayed it wouldn't hit anything, break or fall down. It didn't. I did what my job entailed, filed a live report into the news and a recording of the picket-line fury. I knew at the time how inadequate it was.

When I think back, it was impossible for any journalist, especially someone as naïve as me, to explain in a news piece the significance of the rift between these tough men who had a shared experience of danger, camaraderie and community.

I feel embarrassed that I even tried. And I had no sense at the time that this division spelled the end of an era, that a centuries-old industry was about to be whacked into the ground, to be built upon by 1990s developer guys in garish braces.

The pit I have written about closed for good in 1991. The Lancashire coalfield is long gone. There are Facebook groups of former miners who keep the memories alive. Some of them collect and restore vintage miner's lamps.

It is a lost world, a dirty, dangerous world, but an essential part of British history. The two things that held together pitmen and their families, solidarity and community, had been torn apart by the strike. It was a terrible thing to witness, and I have never forgotten it.

Lesley Curwen

# Buying a Bike

We went to Woodlands to buy a bike
For Sale in the Free Press
*As New, Great Condition, Hardly Used.*

It was true. He was young,
newly-wed, on strike

selling his life
for a gamble.

Desperation
shook hands, closed eyes
spoke quickly.

Dignity
whispered *head up*.

We did the deal.
It was a steal.

Driving home, I tried to fathom
who I was weeping for
and why.

   Lesley Ingram

# Clover

Barely out of my first pair of shoes and I'm down the pit,
chewing metal, can't see a bloody thing and lumping
around coal dawn 'til dusk is no joke, buggers your knees.
And I've heard what folk say about me, look at her,
dumb ass, dozy mare, thinking the grass is black
and the sky blacker still. I mean, yes, a step up from
the canaries, right bunch of Cassandras, lot of 'em.
Never stop banging on about the future, should get a job
reading tea leaves. Save your bloody breath, I say.
But on they chelp, *Gas! Gas! Woe, woe and thrice woe!*
At least I didn't stay down there, not with my dodgy neck
and those low ceilings. But like I say to my ol' man,
what's the chuffing good of underground or overground
when it's all darkness? The girls'll tell you retirement's
alright, three squares a day, sugar lumps for a little treat,
a lady who comes to give my hair a bit of a do on Fridays.
But what's the bloody use of a ribboned tail, a braided forelock,
when they've heaped coal into my good for nothing head.

Jeanette Burton

Last pit ponies coming off the cage at Bentinck Colliery in January 1972 by © John Robinson, Safety Engineer from the David Amos Collection

# Coal

In the blunted night of the coal shed,
without a torch, my fingers dig
among the coal for the coal.
Hear it scutter into the bucket.
Something else is gathered, uttered
from a darker place where memory digs
and throws its coal into a bucket –
as if a ghost stuttered, spoke.
My father clears his throat, curses
the government: 'Thirty years in Rosewell,
in Bilston Glen, in Monktonhall –
and what is there to show for it?'
And what is there to show for it?
Flattened sites, non-places, absences
surrounded by meaningless villages.
The bars look like air-raid shelters.
'If the shops need iron grilles here,
they'll need them everywhere.
Like the miners of Monktonhall
we'll all know what siege means.'
I stumble from the dark into the dark
of that night into this, to light a fire,
to watch the flames rise and flare
into eloquent tongues.

Brian McCabe

# Coal

We waited till the snow had hemmed the house
as high as me, aged five,
ready in wellies and red knit mittens.
Along sacred ground
we rolled his boulder of a body,
me puffing and pushing with all my might,
you letting me think I was pushing.
For feet we saved him splayed out twigs,
a carrot of course for a nose.

I placed him in my ice palace and wept
his loss. Listen, Dad; you can hear the thaw,
two eyes and a smile, there on the lawn.

Julie Sheridan

# The Coal Faces

A miner on the bus adjusts his coat
and this permits the boy to sit beside him
and miners' faces see that he can sit
or go on standing. They are quiet with coal.
*Just mind yer claes* the miner says and leaves him
to fit in, the calculations shifting
on the corners, approximate but still
you don't look round when miners manage home
the way they are and people come to terms
with honest dirt that by the end will kill
his grandfather but it is not his place
to bring that up among the coal faces
that open in bright lines where they were gathered.

Gordon Dargie

# Coal Picking, Broomhill

We are bending over
like men after shellfish.
We dart like birds
in the hard November sun.
I have left the riddle
by a frozen puddle
and we are digging.

The field is turned over,
riddled, left to freeze;
there is nothing here.
A dozen police vans
rumble down the road
towards Cortonwood.
A man throws his shovel
on the stiff ground,
the harsh wind clutches at us.
We say nothing,

yet still my daughter
insists on waking at four
in clenched blue darkness

and downstairs we build
on the floor before dawn
using bricks, people, books, anything.

  Ian McMillan

# Credo

I believe in the blackbird's song,
the sound of clapping
as wood pigeons lift
from the sycamore trees.
I believe in the river's constant flow
water eddying rock, sand and silt.
I believe in the cosmic shift
of a glacier borne rock
from Borrowdale to Crook,
the devil blue stone.
I believe my grandfather's truths
his hands the colour of starlings
from the years he spent on hands and knees
picking at coal seams.
I listen as he names the plants
and flowers in Ragpath Woods,
bluebells, foxgloves and wild garlic.
I watch him collect honey from the hives,
I believe him when he tells me bees are wise.

Rachel Burns

# Dad, 83

He sits in his chair cushioned by cushions.
His breathing, the loudest thing in the room:
the wind whipping hard Monday's wet washing,
gusting through grinding gear, old machines,
petering out airless in the pit yard.
In his throat, and where the coal dust lives,
lining his lungs like dry baking paper,
he coughs, spit dribbles. Grinning, he slips
into sleep. His head drops: ropeless pit cage
hurtling down, telescoped. Tea spilt again.

Alison Tanik

c.1940s Miners waiting to descend in the cage. Photograph courtesy © David Amos Collection.

# The Daughter of a Scab

At school she was known
As the daughter of a scab
But to me she was my best friend

   Rachel Moore


# Deputy Stick

He never shared his worries.
Instead, he whittled
away into the whole yard
of his Deputy Stick.
He hid a silver sliver of mirrored glass
from inside a shattered Thermos
and in those spare snap-tin
moments spent in the coal-dark,
he cut into the skin
slicing splintered shivers
from ash. In time he fine-tuned
the pitman's art and turned a perfect spiral
down the shaft from the bulb to the ferrule.

   Tracy Dawson

Above: © National Coal Mining Museum for England/Harold White Collection

Below: National Coal Mining Museum for England © Unknown

# Digging With My Grandfather: John Richard Evans (19 July 1880 – 9 September 1957)

John Evans, my grandfather, had one brown eye and one blue eye. My aunt inherited brown eyes while my mother got the blue eyes. All of his life he'd lived in Glanamman, a village in South Wales where most went down the mines. I remember him as a smiling, gentle man, with snow white hair and a ruddy, well-scrubbed face. At weekends he wore a dark suit with a waistcoat and pocket watch and a shirt with a collar that buttoned to it.

John's father, Richard Evans, had started working down the mines when he was eleven, but John was allowed to stay on in school until he was 13. He then worked at Gellyceidrim Collieries, where the miners were taken down to the coal surface in a little train instead of a cage. Gellyceidrim was a productive pit so John was always in regular work, except for the big strike in 1926 when everything came to a stop. This lasted from May to December when the starving men were forced back to work on the owner's terms.

There were horses down underground and on Saturdays they were brought up to the stables on the tip behind the house. The tip had grown high from years of dumping stones and waste from the coal. Grass had grown on it so now it was a black and green hill where kids played. On Saturdays, John used to go into Swansea on the bus at 4:30pm. He liked a pint of beer but was never drunk; a godly man, he had a certificate from a temperance society, the Order of Rechabites. He brought presents from Woolworths home for his daughters which they opened on Sunday before chapel.

*

When the siren blew to show the shift was over, the men huddled into the train that carried them above ground, and the heavy tread of their boots and clogs could be heard down the street. He'd get straight into the tin bath outside in the backyard, and Sarah, his wife, or one of his daughters would pour water over him and scrub his back. The coal dust was hard to remove. It hung over South Wales like a pall. Buildings were blackened, sheep were greyed, washing that hung on the line was grubby, and the miners themselves, no matter how hard they scrubbed, retained a grey pallor.

※

Behind John's house, he had a long garden reaching right back to the slag heap, the tip. He grew fragrant gooseberries, raspberries, and blackcurrants. His spade sat in the tilled earth awaiting his return from the mines. Once his long workday was done, he'd go out to his vegetable garden and weed among the raspberry canes and blackcurrant bushes, inhaling their fruity smell and the good air above ground. He was not blind like the pit ponies, but he too felt more alive when he was free and digging under God's sky, rather than in the black of the coal tunnel. He felt so grateful to be there in the fresh air that he burst into song, one of his favourite hymns from the male voice choir, *Cwm Rhondda*.

He died in 1956 when I was eight. I think of him when I smell the sun on blackcurrants and when I dig with his old steel spade.

# Elaine Oswald

© Ken Wilkinson. Photograph courtesy of the
National Coal Mining Museum for England.

# Down Pit

Great grandad left school, to go          down pit.
Grandad left school, to go          down pit.
Dad left school to go          down pit
and plan had always been that sons
of sons of sons would leave school,
walk straight in to a job, go          down pit.
Even when *SCAB* was writing on wall,
when people stood outside dead mines,
families went hungry, people fought, even died –
lads were still telling Careers Officer that
they were leaving at fifteen, going          down pit.
Watching a village die is like watching
a great bird coming to rest, folding its wings
for last time. Shedding feathers, parching
naked flesh, becoming bones, becoming ash.

If you are not from one of these dead places,
it's hard to understand how ingrained
these wasted industries have been,
how deep they sit under skin of generations –
beyond missing fingers, or blue scars
where work got into wounds. Barnsley, or
Sheffield, where steelworks used to be.
People still need knives, forks, spoons –
all those red brick buildings, beautiful still,
despite smithereened windows and skin
of muck. This euthanasia of these dragons,
this quenching of flame, dispersal of men
and women to dole queues, this consigning
of usefulness to nothing. If you are from
one of these dead places, then you will know.

Jane Burn

# Every Man was Singing

*'I think of my childhood, it was always as if there was a lustrous sort of inner darkness, like the gloss of coal, in which we moved and had our real being.'*

So wrote D.H. Lawrence in 1929, a year before his death.

Coal has long been mined in and around Eastwood, the town where Lawrence was born. However, it was during the Industrial Revolution that coal mining really took off in the Eastwood region. In the 1860s and 1870s, several new, larger collieries were developed which would form the bedrock of the industry over the next one-hundred years or so; High Park, Moorgreen, Watnall, Selston (Underwood) and the redevelopment of Brinsley. With this expansion, the small settlement of Eastwood expanded into a coal mining town with the building of hundreds of pit-houses; some are still with us today, a reminder from an industrial era now gone.

Deep coal mining came to an end at Eastwood in 1985 with the closure of Moorgreen Colliery, the last of those pits. I did my basic underground training there in the early 1970s. The rate of production speeded up from the 1960s with the full-mechanisation of the industry and by the 1980s just two collieries remained on the old exposed coalfield, the Pye Hill Complex and Moorgreen. The most productive coal-seams were exhausted in this extractive industry, the coal had run out! An old saying is that 'coal is in the blood', well that is certainly true for me! Seven generations on my dad's side of the family going back to the late eighteenth-century. And me, the last link in two-hundred years of coal mining history.

I wonder what old Isaiah would have made of it? He was the Butty at Portland No.1 Colliery near Selston, a gentleman collier, he was my great-great grandfather. He was a middle-man between the coal owners and the colliers, in charge of what you would call a 'small to medium enterprise' nowadays. A fine balancing act was required to try and keep the peace. And my late dad, a senior-overman, who managed to achieve a class one certificate in mining, a manager's ticket, at the age of 25 in 1958. Little formal education for them, it was education through industry, the 'University of Real Life' as they call it. These were a generation of working men who gave you philosophical words of wisdom, many in local dialect, which stay with you for the rest of your life;

'It teks all sorts to mek the world lad'! – 'Watch yu back!' had more than one meaning.

And what of the legacies of coal? Former industrial scenes now transformed, pit sites as new housing estates or light industry and Black Hills turned to Green Hills. These were the old pit tips or 'Dot'ills' as they were known locally. And mining memorials, at virtually every former colliery site, telling tales of close-knit pit communities from times past. Memories, memories, like a half-life of deindustrialisation, the industry gone but the ebbing memories which remain; tales of joy, tears, tension, tragedy, high-drama, conflict, camaraderie and all the leg-pulling. 'Having the crack' they called it, endless stories of coal mining folklore in a time of coal, community and change.

Others turned to the written word or music as an outlet for their talent: pit poets, creative writers, colliery brass bands, coal mining folk ballads and of course, colliery male voice choirs. Uncerimoniously, the singing was in the pit head baths; miners washing the muck from the previous shift away, all in festive mood, scrubbing each other's backs and singing away at the top of their voices at the end of another shift down the hell-hole. You could hear it a mile away! However, perhaps my most poignant memory is of two nightshift shaftsmen, complete with harnesses, singing whilst being slowly turned up one of the Annesley shafts on the bonnet of the cage, perfect acoustics and beautiful melodies echoing up the shaft. Thinking back, I can almost hear it now ...

## David Amos

Written and performed for the Eastwood Collieries Male Voice Choir's centenary commemoration concert at Nottingham in September 2019.

37

# Ferrybridge Blues

after the stinkdamp, the drowning, the darkness,
after the maiming, the striving, the sacrifice,
after the black humour, the pride, the pints,

after the picket lines, the soup kitchens,
after the scavenging for scraps, the pits shut,
after the villages stripped, the families split.

At the end, it's a heaving of lungs,
the choking, smoking, crumpling dust,
rising in a last gasp.

Liz McPherson

# First-Aider, Oakdale Colliery
*For my father*

Once, a miner, unconscious, near naked,
bloody from head to boot, lay pooled in water
and my father's lamp-light.

He searched for the ruptured artery he feared,
found only a cut in the scalp, bleeding freely,
making the water and coal dust sanguine.

He would talk of that,
could tell of his horror then, and his relief.
Others were harder to speak of.

Sometimes a boy or a man broken by stone or machine.
Then a three mile race to the shaft. A team of eight hurrying,
backs bent under the low roof, aching with the weight of whoever he was.

Four carrying, four running beside, taking their turn,
change and change about, until they brought him out,
brought him up and could lay him down.

Sometimes, no point in running.
Some he never spoke of.
Some he never could put down.

David Thomas

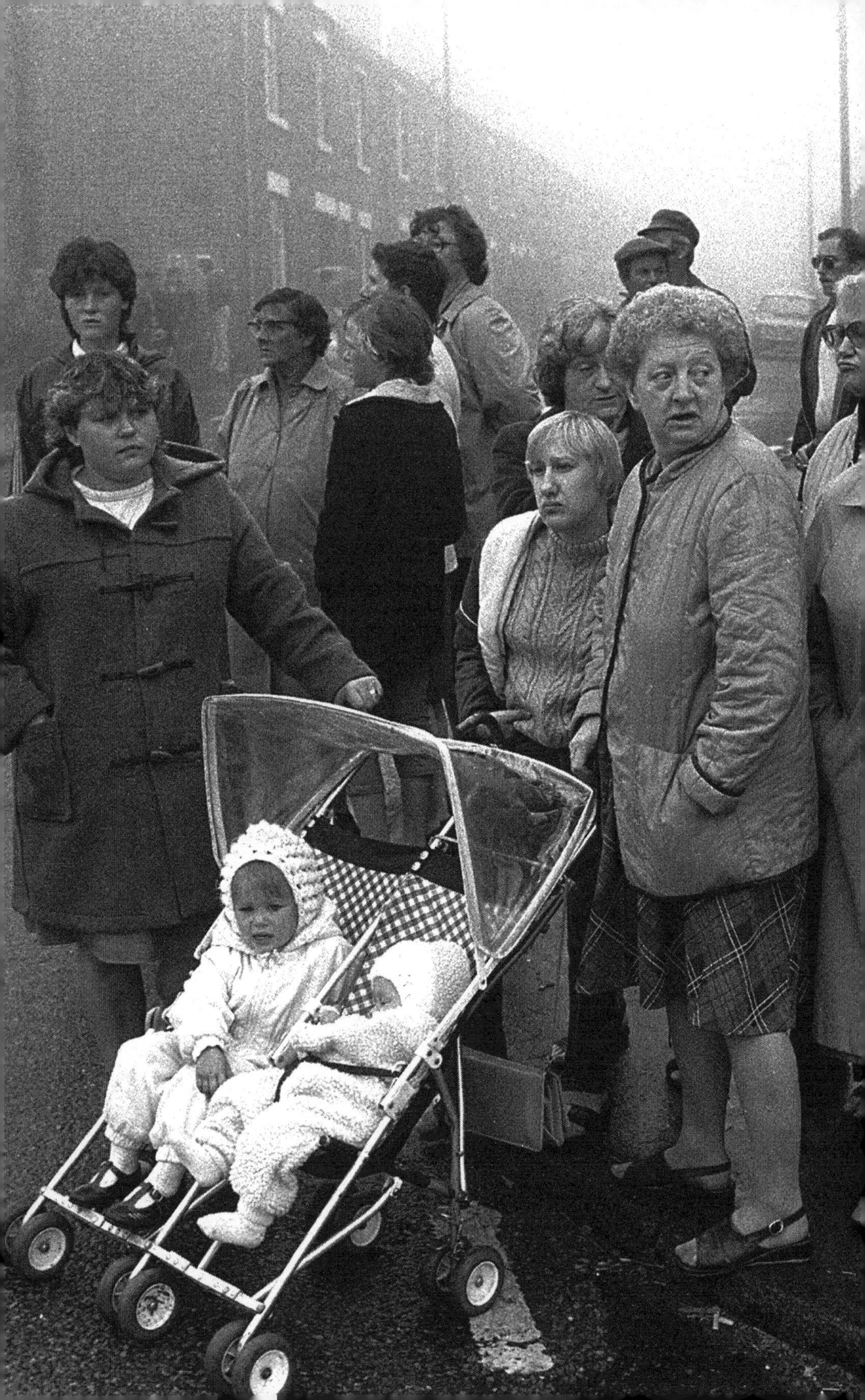

Photograph courtesy © Keith Pattison

# The Flower Arranger

He loves flowers, especially chrysanthemums;
often talks of their colours blinding him
whenever he emerged from the pit
and walked past the allotments.

Every Sunday, he arranges the flowers
in Trinity Methodist Church,
admires them from a pew,
quietly slips away before the first hymn.

Since his wife died, he prefers his own company.
And the company of earth.
His miner's scarf
wrapped round the handle of his spade.

   Alan Payne

# Frost-Gods

An air-berg's exploded!
                              All's
Frost-flak over these collieries, this stubbled corn. –

Tablets dissolve like this,
The only movement: microbe, atom, visible air,
A glistering, getting nowhere.

It is a place I can stand
More than most.
                    I look it over, find
Grey cress on the pond,

Streaked water in ruts like inlaid lead.
I see how progress re-settled Denaby,
Slag-heap, wheel, chimney, a mile away –

And here, how thistles have settled what they can.
Behind me, the river
Rattles through its weir like marbles,

The canal's peaceful and oil-skinned;
                                          and ahead,
The hum of Old Denaby
Carries tree-boles like football-studs,

Like warts.
        – I look it over , warming
To that grim aura: till I stiffen,
By frost, frost-stroke

That petrifies!
            Heritage, home-truth,
Out of control!
            Whose breathings are they,

Who visit, looming
Like Histories from blizzardous homes, clan-clamps of January
To a stand-still here?

All's apparition,
Settled by Danish brain,
Of stag-wood, fiord and conifer, eider-skies

Of Odin.
        Now in their shimmer of stoat-fur,
Clinging mould of fridges,
I see the through staring blains –

Jacks-of-all-Winters, born to embroider,
Born to age meadows,
Scare geese from whitening marshes,

Ford the North Sea and haze
Into England.
        There should be ram-horns, a-hoyes of gannets,
But their adventures are silent:

They're not civil,
Not righteous or malevolent,
But energied with Reverie,

With Operation –
So build fires, invent embodiments and names
For shock meetings

Such as this, as Northness stands
Holding its thistling easterlies in one inescapable
Hush!
    –And naming them,

Begin worship,
By exhilaration and the brain's flickering charms.

Ten seconds, and Imagination's

On hard ground: like a shrub, it has put forth
Berries.

    Its humours

Have adored. –
            Returning to narrow streets,
Their windows draped with poor gauze,
And my father before his fire,

I leave Old Denaby waiting for snow,
Its thistles hardening to the root, its hump
Arching like a white stoat.
                  And I fancy

The frost's blur of grey-midge over that pond,
And Denaby's chimneys smoking gently like snuffed candles.

## Harold Massingham

## I Have Loved Coal

Like a teenage girl loves an older guitarist
with a rough black smudge of eyeliner.
I have built my life on it,
screamed down decades for it,
COAL NOT DOLE – bared my soul for it,
but old women gossip about the pit.
I know the world has had enough of it.

Coal – with its head full of history,
strong arms, filthy engines, heavy,
the small-town sex of it.
Broken bodies, white knuckle wives,
the silence of canaries – has risen
from slag heaps and pit heads to thick air
spluttering into anyone born
late with an old miners' lungs.

I have loved coal, but recently,
when I sit in the fresh place built
on the scar of my grandfather's pit,
I have loved birdsong, greenspace,
the safety and hope of it –
wind turbines, rising white beacons,
sharp armed, slicing clean paths
to a future.

    Emily Cotterill

Copyright © Sarah Wimbush, Rita Besford (white turban)

# 'I thought I might tell you my story'

I thought I might tell you my story, told, coming from a mining family in a mining district.

I lived the first 22 years of my life on Woolley Edge, with Woolley Edge drift mine on my right and Haigh and Woolley Colliery on my left. The sound of Woolley Colliery (totally misnamed, because it should have been Darton) 'buzzer' marking shift change.

My life was idyllic, surrounded by love, care and friendliness. Rationing didn't affect me too much as we grew lots of fruit and veg in our huge garden and my grandma had some magical power to change three cabbages and a few turnips into 4lbs of sugar and make trays of brittle toffee. We kept hens and a pig and periodically we would transport an 11-week-old to the butchers, and he kept half and we got the rest. Officially three months in Wakefield jail for that.

My step grandfather was an ex-miner. His father died in a roof fall when he was 13 and so his mother sent him off to Woolley colliery and he started a 53-year sentence down the pits. He started as a blacksmith's runner, taking pick heads and refurbished filling shovels to the various coal faces. He moved on to a tub helper and finally a hewer.

He was a beautiful man, kind, knowledgeable, thoughtful and a mine of information. Crippled by mining he sounded like a worn-out steam engine, even on a clear day. In a November smog it was painful to see and as I sat with him, I would cry for him. With his shirt off in the summer he looked like a 'join the dots book', his skin covered in flecks of blue and black dots of coal shards.

I never queried at the time why he loved me so much, it was only later in my life that I found out that in his first marriage his wife and his little boy, Wilfred aged 3, had both died of Measles. I became Wilfred.

My father worked at Haigh pit, starting as a pump man, then face worker then shotfirer then a deputy.

What was I going to do – I was going to be a miner and I told my grandad so – I remember he sighed. He said he would have a word with my dad. That's good I thought. So in Barnsley Feast week during Haigh pit shut-down I was suitably attired for my life in mining. Clogs, hat, boiler suit and lamp, best have some gloves on as well because your hands are soft said my dad.

We jumped on the conveyor and rode for a good 800yds, I jumped off when told. I bumped my head on a roof support and I was reminded to watch the roof height. We started to bear right and as we walked along I was now stooping, another 200 yards and I was bent right over. We turned a sharp corner round a collection of big machines, with men working on them. 'Hey up George you got a new recruit?' one of them shouted, my dad replied 'sort of,' and we carried on. Now we were on all fours with about 3ft of headroom. At this point I wasn't quite as keen as I had been but as we made a left turn we now were on a downward slope and I had water up to the tops of my clogs and wet knees. The roof went lower to about 2ft 6" and the water about 9 inch. There was a huge loud crack and my dad turned and asked me if I was ok. I said I had seen and heard enough. There was just enough room to turn round and he led me all the way back out.

Mining was *not* for me.

The real truth of that was that he'd taken me, on Grandad's advice, to the Kent seam, the worst seam you could ever imagine. Full of faults which cracked and groaned and water, lots of water. Adrian would never be a miner if Grandad had anything to do with it. He was right, I never was.

Face work changed from piece work to shift pay and as a Deputy that made life almost impossible. If miners didn't fancy working, then they didn't have to, they got a shift pay and could make up their wage another day. My dad knew he had to leave mining and so he bought a chip shop.

During the miners' strike quite a few pleaded poverty but there were families who were really on their uppers. My mother visited three families and spoke to the wives, she told them that we would give them free fish and chips on Wednesdays and Fridays as long as they kept it quiet and whoever came to the shop brought a £5 note with them. A child would appear at the counter and the fish and chips dispensed and a £5 note handed over. The child would get an envelope with the 'change' inside (£5) and no one in the shop knew and no one got embarrassed.

When my mother died, far too early, those same women came to her funeral.

There were lots of stories about what went on behind the scenes in the miners' strike, some like our story and some very unpleasant happenings never broadcast by the media and never investigated by the police. But that's water under the bridge and long gone now.

My dad died not long after, missing my mother, tired of life – so sad.

*Postscript:*

A few small anecdotes on life with Grandad, you may have gathered that I spent a lot of time with him.

We installed a seat at the roadside to sit and watch the birds flying in and out of the fields and woods. Only a few cars and coal lorries at that time. He knew every type of bird and animal, some by their Latin name. Every tree and bush, when it flowered what colour it would be. Grandma would send us out for 'things', comfrey leaves, elderflower, wild garlic, and lots of other things. Grandad knew where to find them and what they looked like. Grandma had a 'black book' of potions and poultices, and she would ask me whether my dad's knees were bad or not and if they were she would make special comfrey pads for him to bandage on his knees – and they always worked. Grandad's speciality as a collier was spitting. We would hold 'how far can you spit' competitions. Well out of the sight and sound of grandma who would roast us both for it if caught. He always won unless he cheated and let me win.

A miner for 53 years who didn't get home coal – what an effing disgrace, so we used to go to Woolley Edge pit tip and pick coal once or twice every week right throughout the year and by the time winter came he had a huge stockpile to last throughout the winter. All brought home on a homemade trolley made out of pram wheels. The pit had been owned by the much renowned and feared Auckland brothers. Five brothers who made a small fortune out of mining without ever getting their hands dirty. I remember when no one had a car Hubert Auckland had a brand new Triumph Mayflower in powder blue, it was a beauty.

In 1958 my dad was fined £5 (a fortune) for having his load of home coal delivered to Grandad's.

My last anecdote goes like this. For 8 weeks I had to practise 'silent breathing', a method of keeping Adrian from talking for 8 weeks. Hold your mouth in a circle, straighten your tongue and breathe slowly. Grandad told me to get up extra early that coming Saturday morning, I was 10 at the time. Walk along to his house and remember the silent breathing. We went off into the woods and as we went he cut bracken leaves, we lay down behind a fallen tree and put the bracken on the tree. In about 40 minutes along came a mother badger with 3 cubs, they played in front of the tree in a small clearing. Chasing each other squealing and growling, rolling over and over. Mother badger started making noises and they all walked back the way they had come. A sight I shall never forget.

As a PPS I left school at 15 and on my mother's say so went to sea with her brother as a deckhand on an oil tanker. I loved it, I learned more in that year than I had in 4.5 years at grammar school. I should have stayed at sea and made my life there but instead became a Telecomms engineer and got a BSc in Telecomms Engineering – isn't life strange.

Adrian Buttree

## In the Boat House

My eyes adjust, temperature drops, empty
boats dip. I gaze at the mirrored water
tangled in the canvas awning of the roof,

laughing and shifting. I sit in the burden
of the boat, gripping the gunwale as we
pull out, oars sweeping stroke after stroke,

my father's strong back, cotton motes
falling from his white shirt, coal dust floating
in the air, as he reaches out for something.

John Whitehouse

# Jam Butty

Of the days when my Grandad
Came home from the pit
Before he stopped going at all

There is a time I remember
A nugget in the dusty slack

His snap tin
Dull gun metal tarnished with black air
The shape of an arch
It opened like a door.

Uneaten bait.

A remnant of warmth,
The last sigh of a still heat
From 2,000 feet below

Hardening bread
Bitter crust
Red seeded centre like a sweetheart kiss

And something else,
Thin, metallic.

Like blood in the mouth

  John Chambers

# Left Behind

Wunt that when you got kegged, Shay, down the Cundy?
Aye, they kegged us then drove off, like,
with me jeans and me new Nikes.

Do I know what it means, asks Carl,
who grew up here too
with hardwearing revenge

on streets that fell only
from the clash of pans and hot fat at Geordie's
to the black-spoil, iron oxide beach.

In the news: ten million for a new station,
significant opportunities for east Durham.
The lads don't see the point: nowt there,

just them voices chatting all day,
the clipped language of the tannoy with nothing
to say to them.

It was better before, when it was Pit Wheel Field,
blue sky space to ride, when all they needed
was a bike track, jumps high as a house, can of pop, wheelies.

Now, their dreams are unreachable: a pool table,
a place to be where they don't get patted down by police
every single week for fitting the description of dealers.

Aye, they get the train to the match some Saturdays.
They puff up at how many times they've swaggered past security
into Flannels in Sunderland to stroke the Burberry.

Riley says you can buy a house at sixteen,
fake lace curtains painted on boards,
Gas Can Bri swaying outside, cadging fifty ps.

They count the knives as they hustle home
straight down the middle of the road,
dodging lads who've grassed their way out

of HMP Deerbolt to wash in and out the numbered streets.
Troy pauses as the others leave, tells me canny shite
is a compliment really.

## Katharine Goda

Police and striking miners at dawn, Lea Hall Colliery, Rugeley B Power Station, Staffordshire, in the first weeks of the Miners strike. Welsh NUM pickets © John Harris/reportdigital.co.uk

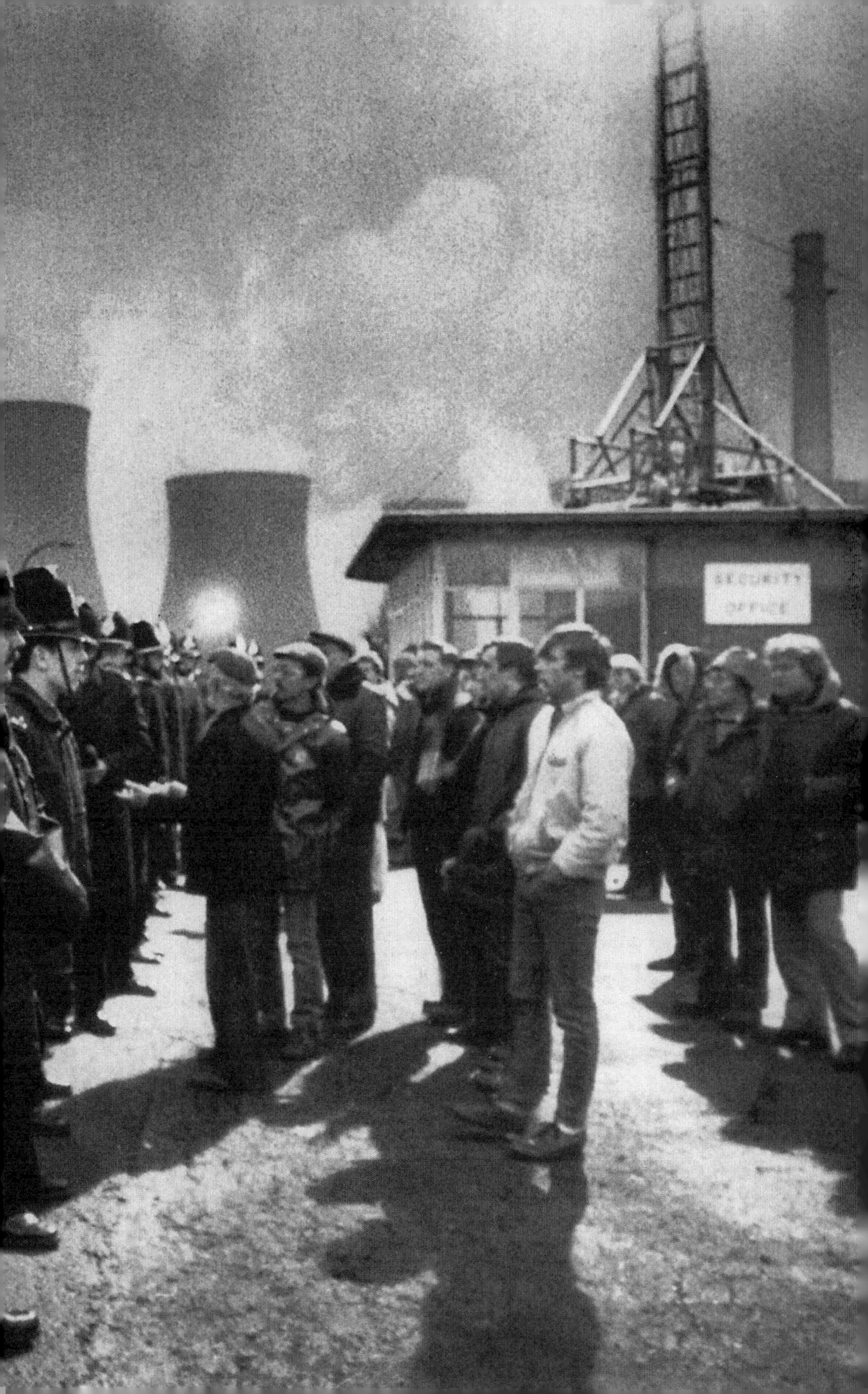
SECURITY
OFFICE

# Lisa's Homework
*Ashington, 1984*

Geography
What effect did increased demand for coal, following the Industrial Revolution, have on east Northumberland?

English
Underline the nouns in the following passage: "It's now or never for Britain's mineworkers. This is the final chance – while we still have the strength – to save our industry."

History
Name an occasion when a British government introduced a policy that improved employment opportunities in the north-east of England.

Science
What is the difference between a piece of coal and a diamond?

Mathematics
If a town has six collieries, and you close all of them, what do you have left?

Joe Williams

# Memorial

The kop chants scab
like it does each time
we play this fixture

though most of them
weren't born
when it all kicked off

maybe we need
to move on and forget

the coppers
waving fistfuls of fivers
at Christmas

and all the
rest of it

either way
there are names
to remember

| | |
|---|---|
| Barnburgh | 1989 |
| Bentley | 1993 |
| | |
| Cadeby | 1986 |
| Cortonwood | 1985 |
| | |
| Darfield | 1989 |
| Dodworth | 1987 |
| | |
| Manvers Main | 1985 |
| Orgreave | 1981 |
| | |
| Wath | 1986 |
| Edlington | 1985 |

maybe
whatever year
you were born

it's too much
to forget

## David Harmer

# Mining

Dad didn't know Greek or Latin
his metaphor's his own – forged
between the shovel's thrust and furl
the first thought and the last –

men shouldering the dark
line of the tunnel, hustling
the hump and fold of the other
the stink of fart and sweat.

That's nice he said of my poem,
his eyelids crinkling with dust
as he heaved the sponge
across his smiling face.

We watched the black coals tumble
into the hot palm of his grate;
centuries of darkness caving in
to fierce flowers of light.

Now there's a poem, he shouted
and flung out his arms and danced.
I thought of the long wrestle
the tussle to turn coal out.

A bit like a poem I said.
That was the last time we spoke.
Now, as I sit in the dark,
my fingers fumbling for the keys

like a miner groping along
the dark coal bed of seams
going for that sudden rush
of daylight at the tunnel head

I think of him, that man

who first taught me to sing.
My father, his buckled stance
from crawling through mud and rain
hallowed be his name.

Harriet Torr

# Most likely a Part of Astley Deep
*(owned by the Ashton Brothers)*

Describing his burns from the waist upwards
for the benefit of readers of the Ashton Reporter
when he was working at Town Lane Pit
in Dukinfield, George Eaton, then aged 14

explained the agony of having daily dressings
applied and then replaced by Nancy Spragg
and how he wished for death, if death were
available, to relieve the pain of being flayed

repeatedly

It happened again to George, five years later

He survived and thanked Nancy
for her services. She did her best
and, according to George, 'was a nice lady'

The article mentions the use of lime water
and oil as an alternative treatment. After twelve
days there is some improvement and the hurt
diminishes. The screaming stops, at any rate

Another method, involved applying tar
but George was spared this. I've tried
to determine the ownership of the Town
Lane Pit, but it makes no difference really

I doubt to anyone

   Steven Taylor

# *from* All Hell Broke Loose – the Miners' Strike, the Battle of Orgreave and the Consequences

In the spring the government provoked the strike by announcing the closure of Cortonwood colliery, a profitable pit with a future. They tore up the existing agreement knowing that NUM reaction would be immediate strike action.

I got a phone call "Ay up youth, get up here this is important". As I nursed my old banger of a car into Yorkshire in March 1984, I met coach loads of striking miners heading out to picket. The strike was on. I photographed it from day one, on and off for the entire year. The mission of the small (but rather prestigious) agency (Report/IFL) I had just been invited to join, was to "show what was wrong with the world so that people of goodwill would do something about it". I have held to this mission all my professional life.

The challenge for the NUM was Nottinghamshire. The 1974 – 79 Labour government had introduced a regional pay scheme that did much to divided coalfields. Notts "easy coal" fed the power stations, its miners paid more than many others. There was less of a sense of community, they had been repeatedly reassured their jobs were safe and hadn't really heard any arguments to the contrary.

They were initially slow to join the strike, but with 20% of Nottinghamshire pits out, the Nottingham Post reported small groups of pickets were succeeding in persuading more Notts miners to join the strike action. Prime Minister Thatcher was alarmed. Police were deployed from all over the country and Nottinghamshire felt like a police state. A vast network of roadblocks on motorway junctions and rural roundabouts sealed off the county. Thousands of pickets were turned around or funnelled into a trap, arrested and criminalised.

### *The Battle of Orgreave*

Coke from Orgreave had been ordered to recommence steel production at Scunthorpe. There were no roadblocks stopping pickets getting to Orgreave, quite the opposite. Miners in trainers, jeans and t-shirts were helpfully directed by police into a stubbled field nearby.

I attended 3 three mass pickets at the Orgreave coke works near Sheffield. At the first I was corralled behind police lines on pain of arrest "for my own safety". I saw the first use of riot shields in an industrial dispute but could see little more than injured & arrested pickets. As one was dragged past, he shouted "You want to get thyself up there and see what's really going on!" From then on, I was in with the pickets.

The second was a similar experience, but nothing prepared me for the final mass picket.

## *18 June 1984*

There were no roadblocks stopping pickets getting to Orgreave, quite the opposite. Miners in trainers, jeans and t-shirts were helpfully directed by police into a stubbled field nearby.

After a ritual push against the police lines, the build-up of attacks on the pickets commenced, snatch squads ran out into the crowd, bashing & arresting pickets. The din of police beating their batons on their line of long shields to the shout of "Zulu! Zulu! Zulu!" would reach a crescendo, the phalanx would open and mounted officers would charge.

In what seemed to be a lull and like many I left for a comfort break. On my return all hell had broken loose. Apparently the pickets had again been attacked and driven down a railway embankment or over the bridge into the terraced streets.

The last charge by mounted officers knocked me off a wall backwards onto a concrete paved front garden as they galloped up the road clobbering whoever they could reach. Short shield units ran past, chasing pickets through the backs of the terraces.

I gathered my cameras and took a risk crossing the police line of long shields that had now formed. I shot a sequence as a senior officer ran past me and started belting a bare-chested youngster with a baton over a car bonnet, forcing him to hop along on one foot back to the lines to the sound of their laughter.

I had not checked my kit after my backflip - that camera was on 125th of a second with a 200mm lens - so that would be two stops overexposed with camera shake and subject movement. I was now in great danger, short shield units and mounted officers were everywhere wielding their batons with abandon.

I shot a couple of frames, got away, came back, shot, got away, came back. I was running out of film in all three cameras. Film was going to need changing and I couldn't stop to do so. I dodged round trying to keep shooting. Ahead some pickets were behind a low wall in a gap in the bushes. As I reached them I found a colleague trying to help an older picket on the ground who looked in a really bad way - they thought he was dying.

A woman started shouting "Get an ambulance!" to the police. The horses swung round and charged. "I'll have you as well, you bitch" shouted one officer as he took a swing at her head. I shot two frames as the miner behind her pulled her back by her belt and the blow missed. It could have smashed her skull. I escaped and changed films.

A standoff ensued. A nearby scrapyard supplied a burning barricade and the pickets embedded sharpened wooden stakes into the road in symbolic defiance. Gradually the pickets dispersed.

I got home later to watch with disbelief as BBC News famously reversed the footage in their headline reports. As police footage later proved, the mounted officers had charged repeatedly before any retaliation by the pickets, yet the reversed footage reinforced the ongoing campaign to depict the miners as a violent mob of insurgents against The Rule Of Law which required an escalating response by hard pressed officers etc. The rest of the main stream media (MSM) also put the blame on the pickets. The Home Secretary mooted life imprisonment for the "rioters". Years later the BBC admitted it had reversed the footage – but claimed it was a 'mistake'.

My picture of the attack on Lesley Bolton was used across almost the entire front page of Labour Weekly and subsequently by alternative other left media, many unions and publishers abroad. It appeared on badges, banners and posters. It became emblematic for the coalfield communities of the way they were being policed.

The blurry image of the lad being assaulted over the car bonnet was reproduced by Stern magazine in Germany over a double page spread to great effect with the caption "In Germany we do not beat our trades unions, we incorporate them".

A year later and largely unreported by the MSM the trials of 79 pickets for "riot" at Orgreave collapsed. Not only had officers made up or had their statements dictated to them but the existence of a new secret police manual emerged. The purpose of the long shields, the drumming of batons, the short shield units, the police horse charges and snarling dogs, was firstly to intimidate, to install fear in the crowd and secondly to 'disperse and/or incapacitate'. 8,000 pickets had faced 10,000 riot police. Had substantial portion of the 160,000 miners on strike got to Orgreave it would've been a very different story. In any event the convoys of coke lorries ceased that day.

Almost immediately after Orgreave, attacks on pit villages the heart of the strike in Yorkshire commenced. The same style of policing and indeed journalism was applied. I would listen to the reports of the event I had just covered and hardly recognise anything.

Whole pit villages would be sealed off in the early hours. You couldn't get in or out. The strike breaking force of police took on whole communities, just to get a couple of broken men into a pit employing thousands.

Day after day I attended picket lines where hundreds of strikers would emerge from the darkness having walked miles across the fields to help evade police cordons.

For me the early hours meant getting close with a wide-angle lens and a powerful flashgun. I dodged the batons. I used to pray for dawn... for some light. It became a winter of increasing fear and exhaustion. The policing made it unsafe to travel alone.

John Harris

# LABOUR WEEKLY

LABOUR'S OWN NEWSPAPER no 642 June 22 1984  40p

## Day of action is called for June 27

ALL out behind the miners is the rallying cry from Kent NUM.

Kent NUM has called for a day of action in support of the miners for next Wednesday, June 27. Organisers expect widespread stoppages in the south east area and expect thousands to join a demonstration in London.

Already building workers, dockers and London Transport engineering workers have pledged their support.

Stoppages are also expected among local authority direct labour work forces and on road and railways.

Demonstrators are being asked to wear black arm bands in remembrance of the two pickets who have lost their lives since the dispute began.

Malcolm Pitt, president of the Kent NUM, said: "So far in the dispute we have received magnificent financial and moral support from the trade union and labour movement, but now after four months of struggle we need the active participation of workers and we are calling on them to strike in the south east for one day in solidarity."

"We feel that the dispute has gone beyond the question of pit closures. The government has turned it into a trial of strength not only with the NUM but with the entire trade union movement.

Assemble 1pm Tower Hill EC3, March through Fleet Street, rally Jubilee Gardens 3.30pm.

## Go in and hit them hard

VIOLENCE at Orgreave was engineered by the government, says South Yorkshire's police boss.

"No one was stopped from going to Orgreave," says George Moores. "They wanted to get them all together and have a real go at them.

"The government has declared a class war. It wants to drive the working class into submission in this area."

Moores, who chairs South Yorkshire's police committee, concludes: "The government engineered that confrontation.

"The crime should be laid at their door. Their message to the police was 'Go in and hit them hard'. The use of dogs and horses was terrifying."

Moores accuses the government of "wanting the working class to get a good hiding and be beaten into submission."

"They wanted Orgreave to be a media spectacle and then blame the violence on pickets."

Moores was with home secretary Leon Brittan at the time the clashes between police and pickets took place outside the Orgreave coke works, near Rotherham. He pleaded for the plant to be closed.

"I knew that the pickets were getting a good hiding, but Brittan refused and talked about free trade."

■ There were 79 reported injuries in Monday's clashes — 51 pickets, including Arthur Scargill, and 28 police.

JOY COPLEY

*Splendid! We put Ian MacGregor in charge of the post office and bingo!*

Picture: John Harris (IFL)

## She was only trying to help . . .

LESLEY Boulton lifts up her arm to protect herself from a police baton, *writes Joy Copley*.

Her crime? She was trying to help a picket with crushed ribs outside Orgreave coking works.

"I was trying to keep out of the way and was stood on the pavement. I was shouting for someone to call an ambulance for the pickets who had been badly injured. Suddenly this horse came galloping at me and the policeman hurled abuse at me and took a swipe at my head. It was terrifying," said Boulton, a member of Sheffield Women Against Pit Closures.

"The police were completely out of control. They had pushed the pickets right up into the village and were just lashing out and hitting anyone who was not wearing a uniform."

John Harris, the photographer who captured this picture ended up in a bush after he dived away from the mounted police officer who also took a swing at him.

Boulton added: "It was clear to me from early on in the morning that the police tactics used caused the violence. The pickets had not gone to Orgreave wanting that sort of battle."

■ Young miners fight — page 5

# LABOUR WEEKLY Supports the miners
# Never be left without it

Photograph courtesy © John Harris/reportdigital.co.uk

# Pit Closure as a Tarantino Short
*after Ian McMillan*

The Suit who pulled the trigger left
a card between the victim's fingers,
printed white on red.
*Business Closed* was all it said.

He wiped his bloodless hands
down his shirt for show,
as if someone still watched him
as he turned to go. And as he did,

he met the dead man's stare
and noticed how the bullet hole
between those two dark eyes
made up a black ellipsis; then he swore

he heard the dead man's voice
above the heartbeat of the clock:
*Nothing's finished, only given up.*
Before he left, he checked the lock.

   Helen Mort

# Pneumoconiosis

This is The Dust,

black diamond dust.

I had thirty years in it, boy,
a laughing red mouth
coming up to spit
smuts black into a handkerchief.

But it's had forty years
in me now: so fine
you could inhale it through a gag.
I'll die with this now.
It's in me
like my blued scars.
But I try not to think about it.

I take things pretty easy
these days, one step at a time:
especially the stairs.
I try not to think about it.

I saw my own brother: rising, dying
in panic, gasping
worse than a hooked
carp drowning in air.
Every breath was his last
till the last.

I try not to think about it.

Know me by my slow step,
the occasional little cough, involuntary
and delicate as a consumptive's,

and my lung full of budgerigars.

Duncan Bush

# The Queue

Gresford church is hectic with quilts,
tulips and W.I..

Behind the hubbub a fresco stops breath
with rain, charred pit props,
and empty boots.

Receding into the painting's heart, the queue.

Babies in prams
        old men and vicars
                women clutching at children's hands

smaller and smaller they line the roadways
        until no bigger
                than grains of slag.

Below the painting, a book.
Two hundred and sixty six names
… Jones … Williams … Parry … Griffiths …

in thick black ink.

    Robbie Burton

# Scargill

*i*

The dictionary is his Bible. Full stop.

He knows boys who were crushed
with only a handful of adjectives in their tipple tins.

Some words will always be difficult to pronounce:
*Oaks, Huskar, Senghenydd.*

*ii*

He points at the dole-not-coal paddy train,
it will arrive shortly at Platform Do-or-dinosaur.

*Rule 41, rules okay*, he says
the National Executive Committee says.

Inky corridors begin to infect conservatories.

There could be other words, other skies
but his eyes – blue and infinite – have limitations,
*there's one path lads: picket!*

*iii*

Faces crowd into a crown.

Each step up the mountain creaks like a blue back.

He lights the wall of a stadium with his cap lamp,

*the stray-dog-kids are coming,* he says,
raises his iambic voice, that finger.

## Sarah Wimbush

# Thatcher

The day they buried Thatcher
I was standing in the rain
in Goldthorpe where the closures hit them hard.
Someone had made an effigy

and dragged it from the yard –
her handbag trailing and the wig askew.
They pushed her in a rusting pram
past empty pubs and crumbling schools

to where a bonfire waited
on the recreation ground.
And when they lit the newspapers
a groan erupted from the crowd:

men wept with joy, the children danced
and all the women cheered.
The mask slipped first then melted.
The smoke was black and stung my eyes.

Ian Parks

# Scuttle

It had to be rammed,
two-handed, its slanty mouth
shoved into the heaped coal
so the lower lip
chomped through the black cobs
till it gagged
then swallowed.
Then had to be burped,
tipped upwards and jogged
so the nuggets
tumbled and settled inside,
then rammed again,
and with each raid
the stockpile shrugged a little,
faked a mini landslide
then reset,
or stray lumps skittered
over the cellar floor.
Then it had to be lugged
up the stone steps,
airlifted over the front room carpet
and plonked in the hearth.
Till later on
when it put in a shift,
got swung forward
then jerked back,
thrown forward then yanked back
till it coughed up
its black spew,
retched into the fire –
*has it gone out?* –
so the flames in the grate
became thick twists
of phlegm-coloured smoke.
Don't call it a pail
or bucket,

don't use the word hod.
You could gawp
in its big gob,
stare into its depths
and not see the bottom,
a fathomless pit
down there it was,
though sometimes an earwig
or toffee wrapper popped out.
The milk churn
was its soppy cousin.
It dealt in mystical units
of work and worth
called hundredweights.

Simon Armitage

# Six Bells

*for the forty-four miners killed in the explosion on 28 June 1960*

Perhaps a woman hanging out the wash
paused, hearing something, a sudden hush,

a pulse inside the earth like a blow to the heart,
holding in her arms the wet weight

of her wedding sheets, his shirts. Perhaps
heads lifted from the work of scrubbing steps,

hands stilled from wringing rainbows onto slate,
while below the town, deep in the pit

a rock-fall struck a spark from steel, and fired
the void, punched through the mine a fist

of blazing firedamp. As they died,
perhaps a silence, before sirens cried,

before the people gathered in the street,
before she'd finished hanging out her sheets.

Gillian Clarke

# Shopping List

sunflower oil
milk
plain yoghurt
butter
custard*
eggs
bread - the nice one
namak
shakar*
bananas
peaches*
oranges*
tomatoes
lahsun
pyaaz
gobi
aloo (bag of small ones)
chickpeas
dhania
plain yoghurt
palak (big bag)
fish fingers*
tea bags
digestives*
washing powder
toilet rolls
*only if on offer
namak - salt
shakar - sugar
lahsun - garlic
pyaaz - onions
gobi - cauliflower
aloo - potatoes
dhania - coriander
palak - spinach

Safa Maryam

# 1984

*'Soup' kitchen*

This little girl standing between two women
each holding out a plate of food in the Hucknell
and Linby Community 'soup' kitchen is about to kick off.
She doesn't want sausages or steak and kidney pie,
somebody else's food. She doesn't want to be
in this church building with her dad, and other dads.
No, she wants to be home at tea-time with her mum
*We can go to the chippy when your dad gets in*
with her brother in the paddling-pool – her dad,
still with muck on his face squirting them with the hose.
But her mum's out again collecting money. The two ladies
are nice but she doesn't want *their* dinners and her dad
can tell her she should be grateful all he likes but she's not.

*2. Night-picket*

Our village is full of false rumours.
*Nothing going on. The pit's shut today.*
Word spreads. We leave our houses,
kids asleep, our husbands in front of TVs.
We've been serving in soup kitchens,
collecting in union meetings, are not tired,
only more fired up. Women singing, chanting,
ignoring lines we're not supposed to cross.

The copper with no back-up looks confused.
You can sniff one out anywhere and when
they come, as we knew they would, crouching
in Judas coaches, sneaking to a rearranged shift,
we jab fingers at each darkened window
and call them by their true names.

## Pam Thompson

Top: Photograph courtesy © Keith Pattison

Below: Photograph courtesy © Brenda Prince

# Stone

Was there any reason not to commit the crime, having been born into the punishment?

I had to write the poem in the pitch dark, because you were in the pitch dark.

They closed the mines, they did. There was a line of policemen, a line of miners, an extraordinary photograph.

Darkness that is complete rests on your face, the darkness would squeeze the breath out of you, the darkness would enter your mouth, it would reach inside of you.

There are no mines here anymore, but the children of miners sit in the dark.

You inherited darkness, it was something your cells already knew, the darkness knew you when you took your first breath.

And the stones remember. The stones try to tell us what happened. Nothing can thrive there, even the new houses burn down.

You might think the stones would be indifferent to darkness, but they took the sobs of infants into their grain, like a fingerprint, like an impression of ferns and fishes.

A shovel still scrapes when there is no wind, at one in the morning and two in the morning.

## Audrey Henderson

# Survey

A rig has been here for three weeks
drilling pasture beyond The Common
where seismologists caught an echo
of bedrock whose dark-coloured veins
could herald a wealth of lorries.

Headlines in the weekly news evoke
slag heaps and urban discontent.
Readers discuss our country's need
for coal, ways in which geology
could save their lanes and gardens.

It is dawn in a guest house car park.
Engineers meet round unmarked vans
then meet again on site. All day long
they drill and pull the core to surface
as deadlines close on stubborn strata.

In the high country where they live
the football knockout is sponsored
by a City institution. Players train
on land re-claimed from pits, old men
watch, are breathless standing still.

    Oliver Comins

# The Thread

They could only bring the bodies up,
not the deaths on a chain thread
below the brisk, tut-tutting
wheel of the pit-head.

School mornings of incidents
we filed towards classrooms
along corridors flooded with hush, not too young
to be conscious we had come

from homes whose terraced doors
had been mysteriously passed over.
We guessed the dead in whispers
by their missing sons and daughters.

They came back of course, in time,
to all the loud babble of a schoolyard in the sun.
And the deaths were left
like chambers beneath us, sealed up and dumb.

   Wayne Price

# *from* **The Two Magicians**

Nothing to do now but go fishing.
  Sign on. Take the dogs out. Get stoned.
Go fishing. Maggots. Snap. On your bike – free-wheeling
  down the lanes to Ulley, Kiveton.
Or with Grandad on holiday –
Thought this were the land of milk and honey
when I were a boy ... Early morning –
  mist wreathing the lanes near Honiton.

The police waiting round a corner
  near the disused airfield. Acid House
in the distance. In the mirror
  another car stopped. Grandad's torch-lit face.
Daz's *We're going fishing.* Grandad's *Let's go
to that rave!* As they let us go
they're searching these pale faces in the mirror,
  their car pulled over in our place.

...

'Bobbies' him and my dad call the police.
  A bobby in a café in town –
he's dragging this girl by her pig-
  tails, her screams echoing all the way down.
He'd sat beside her. She'd said something.
Her dyed red hair. Dockers. Stud earrings.
Something tightening, like a vice.
  Rising towards us, looking slowly round.

Something rising towards us on the news.
  The enemy within. Coal-black Mick.
Claire's dad arrested, as little Leigh arrives,
  down at Silverwood picketing.
*It took four on 'em to get in the van
–rest to keep t'rest o't'strikers off. Everyone
in* The Joker. *What do I know –
  none on 'em were from South Yorkshire.*

On their new record Johnny Marr's guitar
  on a fierce fuse. I am the sun and air
is Morrissey singing? Son and heir.
   Their benefit concert with The Fall, New Order.
Talking to Grandad about it all –
*God dint make men to go down an 'ole.*

Mick's big hands. Lifting bricks. Fresh air–
  whatever happens he's not going back down.
That girl's screams still echoing – look around
look around look around round round ...
Something rising towards us, now as before.
  Up from The Joker. That bobby's hand coming down.

King Arthur striking the table
  harder, raving and growing more fierce and wild.
New Order: Because we're rebels.
  Talks breaking down. O bide, lady, bide.
Johnny Marr's guitar screaming, echoing –
Mum's *Turn that down I can't hear myself think!*
Two boys on the top of the pile, picking coal.
  Me thoughts I heard one calling: Child.

Paul Bentley

# Valley Funeral

food was left on the doorstep

the butcher put a sign in his shop

and on the day
where what he was
or wasn't were both equal

people lined the garden
and the street
and listened where they could

perhaps remembering
how the banter stopped
as they stepped into the pithead cage

and dropped

or how he set the charges
and once saw a man's moustache
blown off

a shy man
who sang and joked
in the clubs

and how sudden it was

   Hilary Taylor

# Vigil

I arrive in time
to see you slip in and out of sleep,
hair in a quiff like your photos as a boy.

A gouge, blue-black, dug in your cheek,
from days down the pit.
Only salvoes of footsteps,

nurses peer in. Morphine-drowsed,
you mouth the air. I lean in close
*Terry, it's me, your cockney cousin.*

You say *It's only the two of us now.*

*

Thirty years earlier, I wait outside the prefab
in a row cut through the valley, shadowed
by the pit head. A boom shudders the air.

Women spill out, standing on doorsteps.
My Auntie Gladys twisting her hands
in her cross-over pinny. A thick silence,

the noise of an ambulance getting closer,
disappearing. Someone running,
breathless, shouting *only one casualty.*

And you coming home, your face striped
with coal dust, pale circles around your eyes.
You pick me up, swing me in sooty hands.

Judith Wozniak

# Wayside

Walking for hours along disused railway
tracks with my book, my bag of apples,
striding over black oak sleepers, thinking
of trains that carried kids from our pit village
to Cleethorpes, Skegness – as if we too might
be changed into ruddy poster children
grinning against a backdrop of white-laced
waves with picnics, clean socks, buckets
and spades. And loving how tall they were,
the rosebay willow herbs that sprouted
down the edge of cinder tracks – wild, purple,
profligate. I didn't know their Latin name
then – *Chamaenerion angustifolium* –
but I loved how they took their chance,
how coal dust couldn't stop them,
how tangled seed-heads repopulated
fallow ground with such abandon,
how roots struck rhizomes into gravel.
In the south, I'm told, they attract
the rare Four-Spotted Furrow Bee –
*Lassioglossum quadrinotatum* –
but I never saw anything so golden.
Only ants, flies, nameless black things,
hungry, as we all are, for nectar.

Rosie Jackson

Photograph courtesy © Keith Pattison

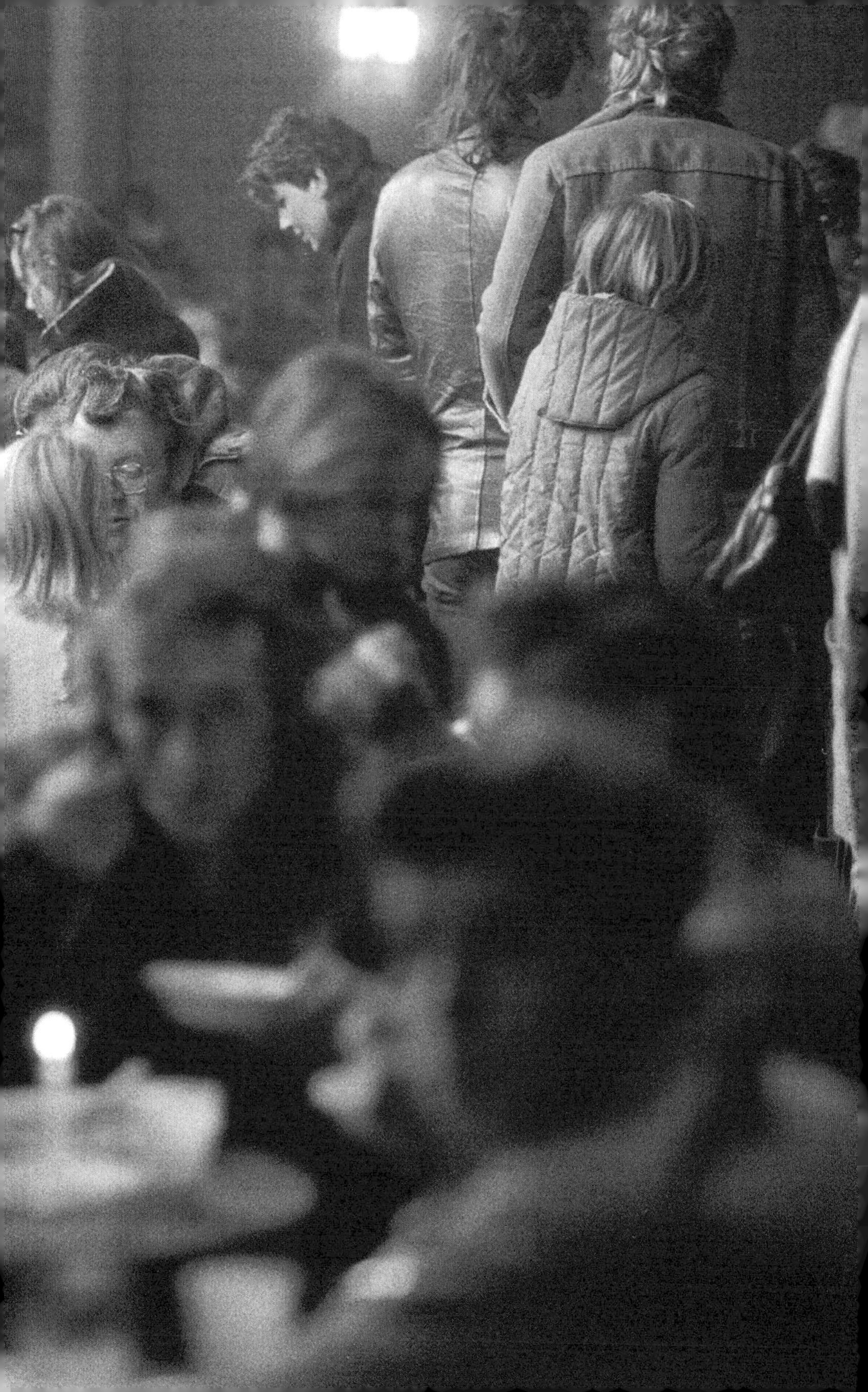

# You Have Got to Stand Somewhere

As a photographic student in the late sixties, I was taught the guiding principle of 'the concerned photographer', Cornell Capa's description of photographers whose ambition with their work was to use pictures to educate and change the world, not just to record it.

It was July 1984 when I arrived in Easington Colliery, the miners' strike had been going since March, but apart from picketing at other sites, including Orgreave, all was quiet at the pit gate. Just a token picket to prevent non-striking members of other unions from crossing picket lines. It's difficult now to remember a time before the internet, e-mail and multiple sources of news. The mainstream media found an easy hate figure in Arthur Scargill, the miners' leader, and mauled mining communities, portraying these law-abiding industrious communities as being gullible and duped, lawless and intimidatory. People just wanted to have a decent job, and few of us would swap places for a night shift digging coal five miles out under the North Sea.

I was a bit out of my comfort zone, I usually documented arts projects, but an organisation I worked for had some spare funding and a contact with the Easington Lodge of the NUM. They asked the committee if they could use a photographer to show a different narrative of life in a village on strike.

Cue some amusement, in those days, cameras were for holidays and nothing else. No one could foresee what would happen to this quiet backwater, but I was welcomed, truly by everyone I met.

It poured on my first day, Dennis Raine and Joe Mather were picketing by the traditional upturned oil drum and blazing fire, rain dripping off their noses ... July! Gently, they said to me that I would make my own mind up, but they would just like me to hear their side of things.

Heather Wood of the women's support group was determined that no one would be starved back to work as had happened so many times in the history of northeast coal mining. I knew instantly this was the place I most wanted to be.

It also helped that Easington was very much, minus the pit, like the close-knit community I grew up in. I felt completely at home.

But there was always the question, where do you stand. Which side are you on? I still thought perhaps I could wait and see. Early mornings at the pit gate, I was lodging two streets away with Micky Barker, one of the strikers, when rumours circulated that political pressure was on the police to get a working miner into every pit.

The stand-off went on for four days. A few local press arrived, they gathered on the corner opposite, behind the police. I stood with the people I was getting to know. A superintendent did me a huge favour when he threatened me with arrest. I was suddenly 'our' photographer. I had arrived, I knew where I was standing.

And once there, how could I leave. Bitter disappointments and betrayals characterised the following months, but also overwhelming solidarity from labour supporters, trades unionists and well-wishers from all parts of the country. No one in their darkest dreams imagined the strike would last a year.

Day by day, week by week, dependent on the generosity of strangers, no money changed hands, no one was turned away, no one went hungry. It was because of the welcome, kindness and generosity of everyone forty years ago that I was able to stay and witness events unfold, acutely aware I didn't have to live with the consequences.

Forty years on, Easington Colliery Club organised a party, as they had on the news of the death of Thatcher. I was really moved by the invitation from Danny, the club secretary. A singer on stage belted out classics, a mountain of sandwiches, and on the screens that usually displayed the bingo numbers, my photographs on a continuous loop. Yes, Easington is a pale shadow of its former self, but there is immense pride in the struggle. An engraved plaque displays the names of the women who, for a year, helped feed and clothe the community.

If you fight you don't always win, but if you don't fight you will always lose.

## Keith Pattison

# Wound Up

*At Kellingley, the last deep coal mine in England, the last shift clocked off on December 18, 2015*

Last shift, winding up.
Half a million years a metre,
faster than light they come
out of the sparkling dust
of ancient ferns, of seeds, of crinoids
pressed thin as frostleaves in the seam;
out of an ancient England,
a polar world of icecaps rising,
falling; a tropic land under a moon
come close and huge;
an England slipping north
on the shift of continents.
up through compacted tailing
of the silt and grit of worn-down ranges,
winding up into light,
into the sky of England now.

Time travellers, they come blinking
at exploding flowers of flashbulb fire;
minstrel-eyed, with red wet mouths,
black faces estuaried with sweat.
They walk heavily like warriors.
Slab-muscled, in filthy orange vests,
steel booted, in buckled metal greaves,
webbing belts, and battery packs
and helmets, here they come.
They could have fought
at Towton, Adwalton Moor, Orgreave.

They check out their brass tokens
for the last time; officially they are alive.
They will check in their gear,
sit in the hot rain of the shower,

and if they weep, no one will see.
They will not say much.

They have been wound up out of history
into this moment. Into England now.
Of the future they can say nothing at all.

John Foggin

Photograph of courtesy © Sarah Wimbush.

# About the Contributors

**David Amos** worked in the coal mining industry at Annesley Colliery, Nottinghamshire, for 24 years from 1974 to 1998, being the last of six generations of coalminers on his Dad's side going back to the late 18th century. After leaving the mining industry, he worked in Adult and Community Education being Project Officer on several heritage projects and a sessional tutor for 17 years.

**Simon Armitage** was born in 1963 in West Yorkshire, where he still lives. In 2019 he was appointed UK Poet Laureate, and is the former Oxford Professor of Poetry. "When I was young everyone had a coal fire in the front room, which meant frequent trips into the cellar with the scuttle to refuel. The area I grew up in was on the edge of the coal fields – a trip to Wakefield or Sheffield and suddenly the landscape changed from moors and mill chimneys to pitheads, winding gear and spoil heaps. I was a student during the miner's strike and the Falkland's War and somewhere in my memory those two bloody battles have become one."

**Paul Bentley** was born in Rotherham. His father was a steelworker, and then a builder, and his mother worked in a knitwear factory. His paternal grandfather was a boxer, his maternal grandfather a miner. His book *Ted Hughes, Class and Violence*, was published by Bloomsbury. His poem in *Coal* is from the pamphlet *Largo*, which was chosen by Simon Armitage as a winner in the Poetry Business Competition, and shortlisted for the Michael Marks Award.

**Liz Berry** was born in the Black Country in 1980. Her work, "a sooty, soaring hymn to her native West Midlands" (*Guardian*), includes *Black Country*, *The Republic of Motherhood* and *The Home Child* (Chatto).

**M W Bewick** is a writer and co-founder of Dunlin Press. He grew up in West Cumbria where his family had many connections to both coal and iron ore mining over centuries. He was a teenager when Haig Pit in Whitehaven was slated for closure in 1984.

**Jane Burn** is an award-winning poet, artist, poet and hybrid writer. She is a working-class person with autism. Her work is widely published and anthologised. Her current collection, *The Apothecary of Flight*, is published by Nine Arches. She is the Michael Marks Awards Environmental Poet of the Year 2023/24. She is originally from the Dearne Valley, South Yorkshire and was a teenager when she witnessed the impact of the Miner's Strike on the local mining community.

**Rachel Burns** has been published in various literary magazines including *Magma, Butcher's Dog* and *Spelt Magazine*. Her poetry pamphlet, *A Girl in a Blue Dress* is available from Vane Women Press. 'Credo' was placed second in The Julian Lennon Prize for Poetry 2021. Rachel's grandfather was a miner from Esh Winning, County Durham, working at Waterhouses Colliery from age fifteen.

**Jeanette Burton** is a poet from Belper in Derbyshire. Her debut pamphlet is published by Candlestick Press. Jeanette's uncle worked at Moorgreen Colliery in Nottinghamshire and her grandmother grew up near Denby Colliery with her sixteen siblings, where they would bake potatoes in the heat from the pit hill.

**Robbie Burton** is the Poetry Society stanza rep for Cross Border Poets in North East Wales. Her pamphlet *Someone Else's Street* was published by Happen*Stance* Press. Robbie remembers blue scars on the forehead of an uncle who, with colleagues from Llay Main colliery, searched for survivors after the Gresford pit disaster.

**Duncan Bush** (1946 – 2017) was a Welsh poet, novelist and dramatist (for film, TV, radio and stage) as well as a translator and documentary writer. Although not from a mining background himself – his uncles were steelworkers – Duncan had a keen interest in the role of industrial work in the Welsh heritage. This was intensified by living in the Swansea Valley, where he was very supportive of the miners during the strike of 1984. His poem here, 'Pneumoconiosis', is reprinted from *The Hook*, courtesy of Seren, and also with many thanks to Annette Bush.

**Adrian Buttree**: My step-grandfather was a miner from the age of 13. My father was a miner when he returned from WWII. A West Riding family for two hundred years with coal in the blood and with two people determined that I wouldn't follow them both down the pit.

**John Chambers** is a poet and musician. He was born in Armthorpe a small mining village. He worked for a time at the colliery as did both grandfathers and his uncle.

**Gillian Clarke** has published two collections of essays, and a version of *The Gododdin*, translated from early Welsh. Her eleventh poetry collection, *The Silence*, was published in March 2024. The poem, 'Six Bells', was a BBC commission to mark the 40th anniversary of the disaster which killed 45 miners in 1960.

**Oliver Comins** recently returned to Warwickshire after living in the Thames Valley for many years. His collection, *Oak Fish Island*, was published by Templar Poetry in 2018.

**Emily Cotterill** grew up in the former mining town of Alfreton, Derbyshire – all of the men in her dad's family were miners until her grandfather left to join the RAF. Her pamphlet *The Day of the Flying Ants* was published by Smith|Doorstop in 2019 and her debut collection *Significant Wow* will be published by Seren in 2025.

**Lesley Curwen** is a journalist, poet and documentary-maker from Plymouth. Her great-grandfather worked in a Welsh coal mine and later in a De Beers diamond mine, where he was killed in a mining accident.

**Gordon Dargie** lives in Shetland and was brought up in Lanarkshire in the 50s and 60s when coal mining there was coming to an end. One of his grandfathers was a miner whose life was cut short by lung disease.

**Tracy Dawson** is a member of Read to Write Balby. Her poems have been published in *Dream Catcher*, *Black Nore Review* and anthologies by Maytree Press/ The Poetry Village, Ripon Poetry Festival and Calder Valley Press. Her father, two grandfathers, uncles, and cousins were coal miners in the Dearne Valley where she was born and raised.

**Jonathan Edwards**'s collections, *My Family and Other Superheroes* and *Gen*, are published by Seren. He grew up in Neil Kinnock's constituency, Islwyn, in the 1980s.

**John Foggin** (1943-2023) was a much-loved poet, who lived in Ossett. His many books include *Much Possessed* from Smith|Doorstop, as well as several titles from Calder Valley, most recently the remarkable *Pressed for Time*, from which 'Winding Up' is reprinted.

**Katharine Goda** is widely published and has received a Northern Writers Award. Her first collection, *Safety Measures Against the Sea* is from Vane Women Press (2023). Katharine grew up with stories of her great-grandfather who looked after the pit ponies at Dean and Chapter Colliery in Ferryhill all his life, and she has relished delivering creative writing sessions in former mining communities in Horden, Easington, Shotton and Seaham.

**David Harmer** was born in 1952. He lives in Doncaster and is best known as a children's writer. He worked for many years in schools directly affected by the coal industry and the strike. A lot of his work for the Grown Ups is published in magazines. He also performs with Ray Globe as The Glummer Twins, often at the Edinburgh Fringe.

**John Harris**, born in 1958 in Stratford-on-Avon, is an acclaimed documentary photographer renowned for capturing the socio-political and economic landscape of Britain from the early 1980s onwards. His extensive portfolio includes powerful documentation of social and political events across the UK, such as the 1984-85 Miners Strike, inner city life, rural hardships, and environmental crises. Harris's work was widely published in left wing and progressive publications and has also appeared in a range of outlets including *Newsweek*, *Stern magazine*, *The Guardian* and *The Mirror*. Additionally, Harris has advocated for photographers and he established Report Digital in the 1990s, one of the first online photographic libraries.

**Audrey Henderson** grew up in a mining community on the edge of the Lothian Coalfield with friends and family members whose parents worked in the mines. In 2001, her family home was condemned after water from disused mines caused major subsidence. Audrey's writing has appeared in *PN Review*, *The Dark Horse*,

*Magma, Gutter* and *The Frogmore Papers*. Her poetry collection, *Airstream*, was shortlisted for a Saltire Society First Book Award. She is a Hawthornden Fellow.

**Lesley Ingram** was born in Doncaster. Her grandfather was a coal washer at Edlington pit, and her Uncle was a miner, who almost lost his leg in an accident at the Yorkshire Main. Her first collection *Scumbled* (Cinnamon) was published in 2015. Her poems have appeared in online/printed journals and anthologies since 2010, and she has appeared at Cheltenham, Wenlock and Ledbury Poetry Festivals. She won the Poetry Society's Stanza competition 2020. She lives in Ledbury.

**Rosie Jackson** grew up in Shirebrook, when the Nottinghamshire-Derbyshire coalfield was active. Although her father wasn't a miner, neighbours and boyfriends were: one of her most formative memories is of going down Shirebrook mine with her father in the early 1960s, crawling on all fours through tiny passageways, shocked by the intense heat. A widely-published poet, Rosie now lives in Teignmouth, Devon, her latest collection is *Love Leans over the Table* (Two Rivers Press, 2023).

**Safa Maryam** is a poet and doctor from the North. Growing up hearing about her working class South Asian grandfathers' connection to the cotton mills in Lancashire instilled an interest in the often undocumented contributions South Asians have made to British industries. She learnt more about the mining strikes after moving to the North East for university, and soon became curious about the role South Asians played at the time in supporting the striking miners and their families. Her work is featured or forthcoming in *Dear Damsels*, *Mslexia*, *Anthropocene*, *Butcher's Dog*, and others. She has been a finalist and longlisted in the Mslexia Poetry Competition. She can be found on Instagram @bysafamaryam

**Harold Massingham** was born in Mexborough in 1932 and died in 2011. The son of a miner, he attended the same school as Ted Hughes and went on to teach at the University of Manchester. His *Selected Poems* is edited by Ian Parks and published by Calder Valley Poetry.

**Brian McCabe** grew up in Bonnyrigg, the youngest of four children. His father worked as a miner in various pits in the Lothians. His mother worked as a cook and a cleaner. He studied Philosophy and English Literature at the University of Edinburgh and worked in various jobs before becoming a freelance writer of fiction and poetry in 1980.

**Ian McMillan** is a writer and broadcaster who presents *The Verb* on BBC Radio. His grandad worked at Dearne Valley Drift and his father in law at Houghton Main. 'Coal Picking, Broomhill' is reprinted from *Tall in the Saddle* (Smith|Doorstop, 1985).

**Liz McPherson**'s work has appeared in a number of online and print zines. Her pamphlet, *Shivering in the Wind*, is available from Yaffle. She worked for a time in mining communities around Wakefield and has family connections to mining in South Yorkshire.

**Rachel Moore** is a poet and writer who regularly holds creative poetry workshops, her work has been published online and her poetry has also been read on the BBC's *The Vibe*. She grew up at the height of the miners strike in a mining community on the outskirts of Sheffield.

**Helen Mort** was born in Sheffield and grew up near Chesterfield, North East Derbyshire. Her collections include *Division Street* (from which 'Pit Closure as a Tarantino Short' is reprinted), *No Map Could Show Them* and *The Illustrated Woman*, all published by Chatto & Windus. Her work has been shortlisted for the T S Eliot Prize and the Forward Prize.

Professor **Elaine Oswald** was born in the north of England. When she was young, she spent summers with her mother's family in Carmarthenshire, where many generations of the family had worked down the mines. Her grandfather's garden is a happy memory, even though the coal tip loomed behind it.

**Ian Parks** was born in Mexborough. The son of a miner, he was active during the Strike. He is the editor of the *Selected Poems of Harold Massingham* and his own *Selected Poems* 1983-2023 are published by Calder Valley Poetry.

**Keith Pattison** was born and worked in the North East. An exhibition of the Easington photographs accompanied the publication of the book *No Redemption* with David Peace, (author of *GB84*) in 2010. Now out of print, a Blurb version is available here; https://www.blurb.com/b/10626753-no-redemption. Other documentary projects include Squatters in Clerkenwell, Teesside Industrial Communities, Newcastle United supporters and 100 Sunderland Library users.

**Alan Payne** was born in Trinidad and came to England when he was nine. A teacher for most of his life, he has published two collections of poetry, most recently *Mahogany Eve* (Smith|Doorstop).

**Stuart Pickford** is the recipient of an Eric Gregory award. His first collection, *The Basics* (2001), was published by Redbeck Press and shortlisted for the Forward Best First Collection prize. His second collection, *Swimming with Jellyfish* (2016) was published by Smith|Doorstop. Stuart lives in Harrogate and taught in a local comprehensive school. His dad was a miner for twelve years in Chislet Colliery, Kent.

Born in Hackney, London, **Brenda Prince** got into photography through her political views. In 1983 she joined Format Photographers Agency, the first all-woman photographic agency and library. The following year she began to document the miners' strike focusing on the role played by women, such as their presence on the picket line, organising of community kitchens and food supplies, and rallying for fundraising.

**Wayne Price** was born in and brought up in the South Wales mining village of Ynysybwl. Both grandfathers worked underground and both lives were shortened by lung disease. He has published award winning fiction and poetry for many years and in 2015 his poetry pamphlet *Fossil Record* was chosen as one of the inaugural publications in the Laureate's Choice series. He now lives and works in Aberdeen.

**Sue Riley** has lived all her life surrounded by a society and landscape shaped by coal. Though not from a mining family, she has taught miners' children in local schools and absorbed the language and traditions that make up a South Yorkshire coal mining heritage.

**Julie Sheridan** was raised on the west coast of Scotland and graduated in Hispanic Studies from the University of Glasgow and now lives in Barcelona. Her work has been published in various literary journals. She won the 2023 Plaza Audio Poetry Prize and 2024 Plaza Poetry Prize (40 lines), and was shortlisted for the Bridport Prize in both years. Her great-grandfather was a miner, cared for by her mother, and later died of emphysema from his time in the pits.

**Russell Smith** is a film maker and photographer from Hartlepool, once in County Durham. His family have roots in the mining village of Blackhall which he recently revisited in the making and production of the feature length documentary, *The Last Men Standing*, which features fifteen ex-coal miners from Blackhall and the surrounding villages, capturing their first hand accounts of the good times, the bad times and the aftermath of the closures.

**Laura Strickland** is a carer and MA student from Yorkshire. Her publications include *The North, Ink, Sweat and Tears, Dreamcatcher, Northern Gravy, Strix, The Frogmore Papers* and *Butcher's Dog*. She was longlisted in the National Poetry Competition 2023.

**Alison Tanik** is a poet, performer and playwright from Derbyshire, with an MA in poetry from the Manchester Writing School. She grew up in a mining village in South Derbyshire and her family has a long history of working in the coal industry in the Midlands, mainly at Donisthorpe and Rawdon Collieries (Leicestershire).

**Hilary Taylor** is a poet living in Devon, with family connections to coal mining in the Rhondda Valley, South Wales. 'The man in the poem was my partner's brother in law, who died not long after the strike partly due to work-related emphysema. During the strike, his wife, Mary, made toast and tea (all she had) for groups of hungry miners.'

**Steven Taylor** was born and raised in Hyde, near Manchester, and now lives in Kilburn, North London. Hyde was built on coal (and cotton) and the poem is part of a much larger sequence exploring the history, culture and politics of the region. He is widely published.

**David Thomas** grew up in Oakdale, a mining village in the Sirhowy Valley in South Wales. His father worked in Oakdale colliery from the age of fourteen until his retirement at sixty five. David became an architect, and now lives in Ceredigion.

**Pam Thompson** is a poet and educator based in Leicester. Her latest collection is *Strange Fashion* (Pindrop Press, 2017) and forthcoming is her prize-winning pamphlet, *Sub/urban Legends* (Paper Swans Press). Pam's maternal grandfather was a miner and she wishes she had known him.

**Harriet Torr** lives in Caithness. Most recently her poems have appeared in *Poetry News* (the Newsletter of the National Poetry Society).

**Zoë Walkington** grew up in Yorkshire in the seventies and eighties. She has had poetry published in *Hinterland*, *Strix*, and *The North* magazines. Her pamphlet *I Hate to Be the One to Tell You This* won the Poetry Business International Pamphlet competition in 2022 and is available from Smith|Doorstop.

**John Whitehouse** is a retired academic. His first collection, *A Distant Englishness* reflects on his childhood in a mining village. The village was connected by road, canal and mineral railway, to the Cannock Chase Coalfields. Life carried on, his father, a miner, died in his fifties. Meanwhile millions of tons of coal were extracted and transported, altering the landscape.

**Ken Wilkinson** worked on the coal face at Askern Colliery, Doncaster, South Yorkshire, and throughout the 1984-85 Miners' Strike, photographed the event from the viewpoint of a striking miner. After Askern Colliery closed, he studied photography at Newport College under David Hurn (Magnum Photographer). He then worked for 26 years as the Brigade Photographer for West Yorkshire Fire Service until his retirement in 2024.

**Joe Williams** is a writer and performing poet who now lives in Leeds, but who was born in the Northumberland colliery town Ashington. He is currently working on a series of poems about Ashington, its community, and the destruction of the coal mining industry. https://joewilliams.co.uk

**Sarah Wimbush**'s collection, *STRIKE* (Stairwell Books), commemorates the 40th anniversary of the miners' strike 1984-85 and was shortlisted for Forward Prize for Best Collection 2024. Sarah comes from Doncaster and her ancestors worked in the coal industry across Northumberland, Nottinghamshire and Yorkshire.

**Judith Wozniak** is a published poet who spent her working life as a family doctor. Both her grandfathers and her cousin, Terry, were miners in South Wales.